INCREASING YOUR SOCIAL MEDIA INFLUENCE ON YOUTUBE

Increasing Your Social Media Influence on YouTube.

Series "Social Media Influence"
By: Aaron Cockman
Version 1.1 ~November 2021
Published by Sherry Lee at KDP
Copyright ©2021 by Sherry Lee. All rights reserved.

No part of this publication may be reproduced, distributed or transmitted in any form or by any means including photocopying, recording or other electronic or mechanical methods or by any information storage or retrieval system without the prior written permission of the publishers, except in the case of very brief quotations embodied in critical reviews and certain other noncommercial uses permitted by copyright law.

All rights reserved, including the right of reproduction in whole or in part in any form.

All information in this book has been carefully researched and checked for factual accuracy. However, the author and publisher make no warranty, express or implied, that the information contained herein is appropriate for every individual, situation, or purpose and assume no responsibility for errors or omissions.

The reader assumes the risk and full responsibility for all actions. The author will not be held responsible for any loss or damage, whether consequential, incidental, special, or otherwise, that may result from the information presented in this book.

All images are free for use or purchased from stock photo sites or royalty-free for commercial use. I have relied on my own observations as well as many different sources for this book, and I have done my best to check facts and give credit where it is due. In the event that any material is used without proper permission, please contact me so that the oversight can be corrected.

Although the publisher and the author have made every effort to ensure that the information in this book was correct at press time and while this publication is designed to provide accurate information in regard to the subject matter covered, the publisher and the author assume no responsibility for errors, inaccuracies, omissions, or any other inconsistencies herein and hereby disclaim any liability to any party for any loss, damage, or disruption caused by errors or omissions, whether such errors or omissions result from negligence, accident, or any other cause.

This publication is meant as a source of valuable information for the reader, however it is not meant as a substitute for direct expert assistance. If such level of assistance is required, the services of a competent professional should be sought.

Contents

Introduction. 7

Chapter no.1 9

Grow Your YouTube Channel. 9

Chapter no2. 17

Content To Succeed at Growing a YouTube Channel. 17

- Funny Animals. 19
- Video Game Walkthroughs 19
- How-To Guides and Tutorials. 19
- Product Reviews 20
- Celebrity Gossip Videos 21
- Comedy/Sketch Videos 22
- Shopping Sprees / Hauls 22
- Unboxing Videos 23
- Educational Videos 23
- Pranks 24

Chapter no.3 26

How to get YouTube subscribers. 26

1. Create consistent content. 28
2. Leverage your channel trailer 29
3. Ask your viewers directly to subscribe. 29
4. Subscription should be made as simple as possible. 30
5. Create engaging thumbnails 31
6. Collaborate with other creators 31

7. Create searchable titles 32
8. Create binge-able playlists 33
9. Engage with your audience 34
10. Use additional social media accounts to spread the word about your channel 34
11. Share what you're working on next 35
12. Tell a story 35
Subscribers add value to your channel 36
Chapter no. 4 38
YouTube stars are more influential 38
Then other traditional celebrities. 38
1. YouTube stars are better at developing relationships 40
2. YouTube stars drive more engagement 40
3. YouTube personalities set trends and shape pop culture . 41
4. YouTube Stars are Masters at building brands 41
5. YouTube Stars are pacesetters 42
Why YouTube Stars Are More Influential Than Traditional Celebrities 43
Chapter no.5 46
More Views on YouTube for Free. 46
Get Views from YouTube's Organic Search Results 47
Increase Views with Your Video Content 50
- **Content that Educates or Entertains or Both** 50
Generating Views from the YouTube Platform 51
Remember to Be Patient. 59
Chapter no. 6 60

YouTube's impact on our society...60

The excellent or harmful effect of YouTube: 62

Chapter no.7 64

Promote your YouTube channel for more views. 64

Increase the effectiveness of your YouTube strategy................64

Tips to promote your YouTube Channel 65

Create captivating, must-see titles. 65

Make your films more visible by optimizing them....................66

Determine what your target audience desires. 67

Become a member of the community on YouTube...................68

Make your thumbnails unique...69

Cross-promote your own YouTube videos.................................70

Google search results that you want to target 70

Organize a competition or a giveaway. 70

- Encourage others to watch your show. 72
- To arrange your YouTube videos, make playlists...............72

Collaborate with other artists and businesses..........................74

For a charge, run a YouTube marketing campaign 75

Share your YouTube videos on social media regularly. 76

Why Use YouTube?...77

Conclusion: 80

Introduction.

YouTube is an under-utilized but compelling social media platform that I'm sure you've heard of. As one of the most prominent social media platforms in the world today, YouTube has a vast quantity of online content on a wide range of subjects. It surpassed 4 billion daily views in 2012. (counting 30 seconds for a view vs. 3 seconds for Facebook). For specific searches, Google chooses to show YouTube results in the search results. When it comes to online searches, did you realize that YouTube is now the second most popular? Given the more significant barrier of entry required for firms to generate premium video content, the billion-user robust platform can be a source of substantial corporate exposure. YouTube video clips carry a lot of clout on social media and are a terrific addition to your entire marketing campaign. According to Mark Fidelman's analysis, YouTube is the most cost-effective social media medium for running regular influencer marketing campaigns. Some of his company's influencer initiatives, which began three years ago, are still paying off. As a YouTuber, you may have learned that the route to increase audience interaction isn't always straightforward. Views are nothing more than a gimmick that delivers a quick fix.

In addition, the YouTube algorithm does not appear to give special consideration to online videos with a large number of views, which goes against standard media strategy. Instead, it considers a user's "session time" (not available to the users). As a result, you must entice the visitor to stay longer on your online video and connect with you in the comments. Doesn't that seem like a lot to ask of your target audience? Allow me to assist you in making better use of the media site platform in this book. It will also help you strengthen your social media marketing plan and increase your YouTube engagement rates.

Chapter no.1

Grow Your YouTube Channel.

No one can deny the rise of video marketing as a company strategy over the last several years. While famous sites like Tok-Tok, Facebook, and Instagram, as well as your website, are excellent locations to invest in, having a YouTube channel may be the best way to market your company, as one billion people view videos on the network every day. YouTube, dubbed the world's "second-largest search engine," can help people find your material quickly and engage with it, provided you know a few strategies and understand the basics of generating creative videos. Using these ten tips, you may increase the size of your YouTube audience.

1. **Create videos based on a single keyword or topic.**

The most straightforward strategy to attract traffic and grow your YouTube following is to focus your video on a specific topic or keyword. Marketers who are unfamiliar with SEO may overlook this phase in the video ranking process. Still, it is critical to include your videos to reach as many people as possible. To locate the most popular keywords in your field, use a keyword tool like KeywordTool.io, specifically designed for YouTube. Choosing your keyword before creating video content is critical because it will help you build the most excellent material possible around that issue. YouTube's closed-captioning feature may be improved by remembering to include your keyword organically in your video material. Once you've picked a keyword, make sure your title and description are optimized by looking at the most popular videos on that topic. If you do this, you'll get a lot more traffic from YouTube SEO.

2. Repurpose high-performing content that already exists.

Of course, creating and distributing excellent material is a superb method to expand your YouTube channel. It's not always essential to start from scratch when it comes to making such things. To make great films, you need to have an abundance of information that's interesting, beneficial to your audience, and actionable. During the COVID-19 epidemic, users viewed 4 billion hours of "how-to" videos in a single year, which is a lot of time spent on YouTube. As a result, creating content that solves problems for your audience is an excellent method to increase traffic. Conduct a content audit to identify the blogs, guides, and other high-performing pieces you already have and consider how you might repurpose them into relevant and engaging videos.

Remember that the most popular YouTube videos are usually between one- and five minutes in length, so don't feel obligated to construct a film or write a novel. Keep it brief and to the point.

3. Engage with Your Audience

A platform that necessitates interaction with other members. If you merely publish videos and don't encourage discussion, you're losing out on an ample opportunity.

It contains the amount of time spent on the channel, the number of views, the number of comments, and the amount spent watching the channel. So, if at all possible, respond to every comment you receive and urge users to interact using audio/visual suggestions. You can also engage with other channels, which could be a company comparable to yours or simply one that you admire. Don't always rely on the audience to initiate the conversation. Engaging your audience may be as simple as asking them questions about the material or as complex as asking them what kind of content they like to see on your channel or what they'd like to see more of. Also, remember to appreciate anyone who has shared your content on YouTube and other platforms. To keep track of crucial engagement metrics on YouTube, consider employing a social content distribution and engagement dashboard.

4. Get Branded

So, even if your content is top-notch, does your channel's aesthetic appeal to viewers? If you want people to subscribe to your YouTube channel, you must seem professional. Improving your company's social branding will help users recognize your content more quickly. So, if you have a blog or a website, you presumably already have a look and feel that sets you apart from other people and businesses. So it's only natural to extend that identity to your YouTube channel. Here's an example from Nintendo, which has 8.12 million subscribers and provides excellent content about games and consoles, including brief gameplay videos and behind-the-scenes clips. Aside from visual branding, don't forget to include personalized URLs in your channel header and create an engaging bio about yourself and your videos.

5. Other Channels Can Help You Promote Your YouTube Video

The capacity to promote information across several social media platforms is one of the most delicate features of social media. Promote your YouTube videos on all of your social media accounts to get more followers. According to the Digital 2021: Global Overview Report, there is a significant overlap in users across social media platforms. YouTube has the highest engagement of all the major channels at over 90%. It's a strong force in terms of marketing and engagement.

6. Social Media User Overlaps

So, what channels are you watching? Facebook, LinkedIn, Instagram, and TikTok, to name a few? There are plenty to pick from, as well as plenty of unique social media video ideas. If you wish to broadcast videos straight to a channel, a preview of the full-length video on YouTube can be a good solution (such as Facebook). Don't forget to post your videos to your blog! It's also possible to use your YouTube channel in conjunction with your podcast.

7. Show Up & Stand Out

It can be incredibly advantageous to personalize your YouTube channel by participating in videos if you're running it by yourself or as part of a small corporation. Putting a face to a brand makes it easier for consumers to identify with you as an individual. This is good news for vloggers, fitness, life, and business coaches, and solopreneurs. Your face does not have to appear in every video you make, but it should appear frequently enough to attract your audience. If you're this type of YouTuber, you should also use a photo of yourself on your channel (not your logo).

8. Post Great Thumbnails & Leverage YouTube Cards

Despite their small size, thumbnails may have a considerable impact. YouTube uses thumbnails in its sidebar to promote other videos; As a result, you'd want yours to be distinctive. YouTube searches are no different.

Videos with a captivating title and appealing thumbnail tend to rank higher, even if the material isn't as important, because they get more clicks (CTR).

Use methods like highlighted spots, arrows, colossal text, and stunning or eye-catching 1 pictures to get your CTR where it needs to be. We all know that YouTube rewards channels that keep their visitors on their pages for more extended periods. People are more engaged with your material if they are watching for more extended periods. (You may use YouTube statistics to monitor how long people spend watching your videos.) You can incorporate links to other videos or similar material at the exact point that consumers drop off by using YouTube cards. You can use a variety of card kinds, such as a playlist, poll, or contribution, and you can use up to five cards for each video, which appear as a rectangular box or teaser in the video's right-hand corner. Users may abandon the video they're viewing, but they'll be led to your other content, which will keep them on your channel and help you rank higher.

9. Push for Subscriptions

As soon as someone subscribes to your channel, you know they are interested in what you have to say. Keep in touch with your subscribers and those who have already done so in each video you post on your channel. Using this link, you may view a list of your subscribers. Subscribing customers should not be bought. As a long-term strategy, this will diminish your engagement and lessen the trustworthiness of your profile. Remember that if you don't urge your visitors to subscribe, you may lose a lot of potential followers. YouTube view time is likely to grow as a result of having a more significant number of subscribers.

10. Increase Your Uploading Frequency

It may seem daunting at first, but increasing your posting frequency to at least one video each week can help you develop your audience. Don't worry; you won't need the services of a design business or a large advertising agency to complete this task. Smartphones today have fantastic video recording capabilities, and applications like Animoto make video editing simple, allowing you to create video content on a budget. The significance of consistency cannot be overstated. Keep your followers informed about when new videos will be released by posting at the same time each day or week. After then, keep to your plan.

11. Become a social video (& YouTube) expert

Video as a content format continues to grow in popularity. According to the report 'The State of Video Marketing,' 86 percent of firms utilize video as a marketing strategy, with 87 percent of marketers reporting a positive return on investment. Marketers should understand the function of video and how to use it successfully across all social media channels as consumers become more visual and platforms like Tok-to expand in popularity. You'll learn how to successfully set up and manage a YouTube channel, as well as build tactics to make your channel stand out from the crowd, with DMI's accredited social media and Marketing course. You'll also learn how to integrate video into your content mix across platforms, how to grow your online following, and how to leverage advertising and analytics to create compelling visual campaigns.

Chapter no2.

Content To Succeed at Growing a YouTube Channel.

YouTube's popularity has skyrocketed in recent years. No one could have imagined how important YouTube would become when it was launched in 2005 with Me at the Zoo. 18 months after YouTube co-founder Chad Hurley aired his zoo trip globally, Google announced it would purchase the site for $1.65 billion. YouTube's power and influence have increased at breakneck speed since then. It is even the world's second-largest search engine, after only Google. Some of the figures are mind-boggling:

1. 1,325,000,000 people use YouTube.

2. Every minute, 300 hours of videos are posted to YouTube.

3. Every day, 4,950,000,000 videos are viewed on YouTube.

4. Every day, 1,000,000,000 mobile YouTube videos are seen.

In 2016, Google commissioned a poll to learn about the most recent YouTube viewing habits. The following are some of the survey's highlights. Online video platforms are preferred by 6 out of 10 individuals over live television. Eight out of ten 18-49-year-olds watch YouTube every month. YouTube reaches more 18-49-year-olds on mobile than any broadcast or cable television network.

In 2017, Google focused on users who watched YouTube on their television sets. Highlights from the research include the following. Most people prefer to watch videos online rather than on TV. Eight out of ten 18-49-year-olds watch YouTube every month. YouTube reaches more 18-49-year-olds on mobile than any broadcast or cable television network. In 2017, Google focused on users who watched YouTube on their television sets. Highlights from the research include the following. For many individuals, YouTube serves just one purpose: to view music videos quickly and easily. Music videos can't be overlooked, though, because there are so many of them! "See You Again" by Wiz Khalifa featuring Charlie Puth has 2.916 billion views on YouTube, according to the Wikipedia List of Most Viewed YouTube Videos, and has recently surpassed the long-time King of YouTube "Gangnam Style." Music videos account for 77 of the top 80 videos on the list. However, YouTube is much more than just a place to watch music videos. Official music videos provide minimal possibilities for influencer promotion from the standpoint of influencer marketing. However, there are a variety of other forms of videos that provide more considerable prospects for marketers.

- **Funny Animals**

It's impossible not to come across amusing creatures on the Internet; Facebook feeds, in particular, appear to be overflowing with them at times. Catnapping videos aren't that popular this year, but people still love to watch cute animals in action. Simons Cat is an example of a popular YouTube channel dedicated to funny animal videos, including real-life animals and animated ones. There are, of course, several severe animal channels, including National Geographic films starring Sir David Attenborough.

- **Video Game Walkthroughs**

Even though PewDiePie, the world's most popular YouTuber, reigns supreme in this kind of video, we couldn't resist including it in our selection. Millions of YouTube channels are dedicated to video gaming since young boys (the most common gamer) were the first to find the site. The top 1,000 Minecraft YouTube channels may be found on a website devoted just to the game's ubiquity. It's common for gamers to record a walkthrough video in which they play through an entire video game while commenting on their progress. As one of the reasons for Minecraft's popularity, filmmakers use the game's ability to be readily modified in their movies, in which they often play as personalized characters. There may be a lot of engagement and even live play sessions between gaming video makers and their viewers.

- **How-To Guides and Tutorials**

Visual (by seeing), auditory (by hearing), and kinesthetic (by moving) are the three sorts of learning styles (by doing). Everyone learns in a blend of these approaches, but most people prefer one method over the others. In their classrooms, good teachers aim to use a combination of all three strategies. While teaching kinesthetically via a video will always be difficult, it is the ideal medium for those who enjoy visual and audio learning experiences. The more kinesthetically inclined may benefit from a well-structured video that pushes you to work alongside the presentation. There are so many How-To videos on YouTube that you're bound to discover something to assist you with almost any task. These videos have the virtue of being essentially ageless; the only reason a video would become outdated is if the activity itself changes or becomes obsolete.

- **Product Reviews**

The Internet has become an apparent source of information for many people when they are contemplating purchasing anything. When they're interested in items, they want to know what other people think about them. YouTube is much like any other social media outlet in this sense. To see what others have to say, individuals tune in to the channels of people they know and trust.

According to surveys, customers are more interested in buying a product if they read a positive review online. A wide variety of products may benefit from using YouTube, but it all depends on what you're trying to promote. It doesn't matter whether it's cosmetics, a vehicle, or a new kitchen gadget; people are more likely to connect to a review if they can see the product in action.

- **Celebrity Gossip Videos**

People's fascination with celebrity gossip is nothing new; newspaper tabloids have thrived on it for years, and even cable television channels are dedicated to it. It's no surprise, then, that individuals flock to YouTube to get their celebrity gossip fix. Of course, many of these films still look like they came straight out of the newspapers.

- **Vlogs**

Weblog, the natural abbreviation for "weblog," is now often referred to as a "blog," however the term was initially used to describe a web-based journal of a person's daily activities. Many folks write about their daily breakfast and what they achieved the previous day, even though blogs have developed since then. There are some similarities between vlogs and blogs, but they aren't the same idea. To put it another way, they're like seeing a movie of your old journal entry. As a result, the material is frequently more engaging since they're on YouTube rather than in a journal hidden under the bed. Unscripted speech and the appearance of an honest peek into the mind of the vlogger are hallmarks of vlogging. They prefer to specialize in a single field of knowledge. In the YouTube community, vlogs are sometimes likened to reality television. You're given a peek inside the daily routine of the YouTuber (or at least as much as they are willing to reveal). Many vlogs' channels have a large following like that of reality television, which has a lot of viewers.

- **Comedy/Sketch Videos**

Many individuals use humor and sketch films to keep their viewers amused. With so many comedy videos accessible online, you're likely to find someone who shares your sense of humor. Among the most shared videos on Facebook and other social media platforms are these hilarious clips. There's a good chance this flavor will become a viral sensation. A large number of YouTube comedy channels have a more significant following than many network television comedy programs.

- **Shopping Sprees / Hauls**

Watching other people buy stuff they can only dream of owning is a favorite pastime for many ladies. When it comes to shoe shopping, is there anything better than seeing someone else go through the agonizing process? They're called haul films because they follow individuals about while they buy for certain things. Beauty, fashion, and lifestyle channels are the most common venues to discover these flicks. Companies interested in influencer marketing may take advantage of these videos as long as the items being bought match the kinds of products that the channel's audience love and want.

- **Unboxing Videos**

Unboxing videos are very much a phenomenon of the twenty-first century. You'd be surprised at how many people like the opportunity to see something brand new being unpacked by someone else. These are both shopping spree/haul movies and product review films bundled into one; in reality, they lie somewhere between the two. Unwrapping the gifts and discovering out what's within these flicks is like the thrill of Christmas morning for a kid. If you've ever seen an unboxing video, you'll know how exciting it is to see what's inside a present for the first time. For businesses, unboxing films may be a powerful tool to influence consumer purchase choices and a lucrative revenue stream. As with other areas of influencer marketing, this one has a great deal of promise.

- **Educational Videos**

We've separated instructional videos from How-To instructions on this page, even though they may educate as well. It's possible to tell the two groups apart because of their size. TED and National Geographic are two of the most well-known channels linked with huge official organizations and offer their material. Educative films are appearing on the websites of companies of all sizes and across all sectors. The second kind of instructional video channel is geared for preschoolers and elementary-aged youngsters. They aim to provide thought-provoking and intriguing videos for their youthful target audience. Another genre that may be categorized as evergreen since many of these videos draw in new viewers and are repeatedly returned. They "decompose" when their educational value is no longer relevant.

- **Parodies**

The popularity of parodies on YouTube makes them a separate category from other comedic videos. Some parody video channels are more popular and skilled than others. Music video parodies by some of the best are usually rather polished in look. When making parody videos, the line between a successful one and one that doesn't resonate with the viewer can be tiny.

- **Pranks**

A decade ago, Jackass made Johnny Knoxville a household brand, which in many ways paved the door for all the YouTube prank videos. Their popularity is undeniable on YouTube as well as Facebook and other social media sites. These films show pranks on friends, family members, and members of the general public. When it comes to turning individuals into social media stars, these flicks are a great option. Video series in which individuals play pranks on one other, only to get back at them in the following video, are becoming increasingly commonplace. There are prank videos for both men and wives. Pranksters' beliefs and those of the brands they work with may not always be compatible, so it's essential to make sure they're on the same page.

Chapter no.3

How to get YouTube subscribers.

Why is it essential to have YouTube subscribers?

Consider your YouTube channel to be your club and your subscribers to be your fans. Subscribers are your ardent followers who have raised their hands to indicate that they want more of your content and that it resonates with them. They've also stated that they don't want to miss a single video to receive notifications. The example of Mean Girls shows how having a following increases social credibility. The higher your subscriber count, the more powerful you appear and the more desirable your channel appears to new, potential subscribers. There are also subscriber benchmarks to meet to improve your YouTube capabilities. For example, if you get 100 subscribers, you can design a personalized URL for your channel. If you reach 1,000 subscribers, you've fulfilled one of the YouTube Partner Program's requirements.

Furthermore, the YouTube algorithm places a high value on engagement, and subscribers involved with you as the creator are more likely to be engaged with you. They'll be the first to see your new material, are more likely to remark (in theory), and are more likely to share it with friends who have similar interests. The more people who engage with your material, the more YouTube will regard it as a trustworthy video and place it at the top of the search results, making it easier for new viewers to find your channel.

Another advantage of participating in the partner program is the opportunity to earn money. Having 1,000 subscribers and 4,000 hours of viewing time on your channel qualifies you to start earning money from the display, overlay, and video advertisements. It doesn't end there: with 1,000 subscribers, you can start selling channel memberships, and at 10,000 subscribers, you can start selling branded products to your followers on your watch pages. Let's look at how to increase your subscriber base organically to reap the benefits of your audience now that you know why subscribers are vital.

1. Create consistent content

Consistency is crucial when it comes to a successful YouTube channel. When cable was the only option, fans made it a point to schedule time in their schedules to watch a show when it aired. They could predict when the next episode would air and invest in the programming because it was continuously broadcast. In other words, network television provided a consistent source of entertainment for those who tuned in week after week to see their favorite shows. And what happens if a show ends suddenly or if the network decides not to renew it? When the CW's The Secret Circle was canceled after the first season, I remember feeling cheated since the cliffhangers I was left with were never resolved. Fans of YouTube creators have a similar devotion to them. If you consistently post high-quality content, it will provide potential new subscribers a reason to subscribe. It offers consumers a purpose to devote their valuable time to your material because they know when you'll release something new. Acculevel, a Rossville, Indiana-based foundation repair company, does a fantastic job of letting folks know they're publishing consistently right in their channel banner. To avoid missing out on a new video from them every Thursday, check out their channel banner if you're not already subscribed to their channel (seen above).

2. Leverage your channel trailer

A channel trailer is a highlighted video that appears on the homepage of your YouTube channel. It functions similarly to a movie trailer in that it allows people to learn more about you. The teaser also serves as an opportunity to inform prospective visitors on when new videos will be released and why they should subscribe. The Grossman Law Firm, an IMPACT client, uses this channel trailer to encourage visitors to subscribe for fresh material. This trailer, which can be seen on their California Probate and Trust Litigation channel, does an excellent job of establishing expectations for the types of people interested in this type of content. Scott mentions the areas of law they discuss in their films, the actual state it applies to, the fact that they generate new information regularly. He encourages anyone viewing this video to subscribe to the channel. Short and sweet, this video does an excellent job of establishing reasonable expectations for the channel's target audience and convincing them to click the "Subscribe" button.

3. Ask your viewers directly to subscribe

Although it may sound cliche, encouraging your audience to like and subscribe directly is a simple and successful technique to increase your YouTube subscribers. Share how much their interaction means to you as a creative to be human and authentic.

Some artists do this at the end of the video, while La-Z-Boy of Ottawa and Kingston in Canada, a previous IMPACT client, has started asking viewers to subscribe in the middle. Their subscriber plug may be found about 1:58 in the example below! They not only encourage viewers to subscribe for additional content, but they also include a graphic to underscore the question visually. As a retail establishment where many consumers see the furniture before buying it, Dave, the on-camera performer, does an excellent job of urging viewers to visit the store and "say hello to him" so he can assist them with their furniture shopping needs. PS: Dave's appearances on the YouTube channel have earned him recognition in the store! #Superstar

4. Subscription should be made as simple as possible.

Make it as simple as possible for viewers to subscribe to your video while they're watching it. Include annotations throughout the video that allow viewers to subscribe by clicking on a button. VidIQ, a tool for growing your YouTube presence, does an excellent job doing this. You'll see in the screenshot below that there's a button that, when hovered over, allows a person to subscribe. Make sure you verbally encourage people to subscribe to your channel in addition to posting annotations throughout your video. A more personal approach to connect with your audience and encourage them to sign up for your newsletter is to employ this method. Make sure to provide your readers with a few options to subscribe to if they aren't ready when you first ask.

5. Create engaging thumbnails

Even though this tip may not appear as obvious as the others, consider this: To make the other suggestions work, you must first get people to notice your material! After a potential viewer types in a search, hits enter, and the results appear, the thumbnail is part of the visual first impression they see. The thumbnail is where you set yourself apart from the other search results and earn the user's attention. This video's thumbnail and title are identical, indicating to the viewer that this video is genuinely about the topic they're looking for. The thumbnail also shows the on-camera talent's cheerful face, dressed in an HVAC professional attire, indicating that this individual knows what they're talking about. They make it intuitive and straightforward to watch if you're looking for information on this subject, and if you're making the high-quality videos you should be, you'll have a lot better chance of gaining subscribers.

6. Collaborate with other creators

On YouTube, there are certainly firms with a comparable audience to you. Their admirers might love your stuff as well. Collaborating with these creators is a fantastic method to reach out to new people and gain new subscribers. Let's take a look at another scenario. For musicians, YouTube is huge, and Boyce Avenue has been there for a long time. They perform original songs and collaborations with other YouTube musicians, such as with Jennel Garcia below. The identical video can be viewed on Garcia's page, so if Jennel's audience weren't aware of Boyce Avenue before, they would now be. Unfortunately, I'm not musical, so I can't imagine it's like to jam with another musician. Still, if I saw an artist I follow work with someone else, I'd likely go to their channel and listen and possibly add them to my list of channels to subscribe to. It's like your best buddy recommending a new show to watch or an extensive network deciding to perform a series crossover to promote another show on their network. The same is true for enterprises. If you completed an interview on another industry expert's channel, you'd get in front of their audience, which would undoubtedly include many people who had never heard of you before. They may be more tempted to check out your channel and even subscribe after being aware of you.

7. Create searchable titles

The title of the movie, like your thumbnail, is quite essential. A good title sets the tone for the video, not just for what it's about but also for what it's about to accomplish, and it encourages people to click and watch. When a creator demonstrates comprehension of the user's search intent, it signifies a deeper awareness of the audience's wants and what they're seeking. To get to the bottom of why you'll have to delve a little further. It establishes trust and demonstrates that you are a trustworthy resource worth subscribing to if they have further queries.

8. Create binge-able playlists

I'm in the process of arranging my wedding. I've never planned a wedding before, so how would I even know where to begin? Enter Bluebird Bride Academy's "Where to Start with Your Wedding Planning" playlist. Lauren talks about how she's organized many weddings before, and she's here to help in the first video, which immediately sets my mind at ease as a wedding planning beginner.

She starts with the basics, then moves on to more specific questions to ask possible venues in the following video. She walked me through all I needed to know, making the process seem less daunting and keeping me on track. You can understand that this bride quickly subscribed to this channel and directed any queries I had to Lauren. I'm not the only one, judging by her over 5,000 subscribers. Playlists provide you the best chance of attracting new subscribers by demonstrating that your material is consistent and directing them on a long-term journey. To keep people interested, you need to include a long-term objective or process into your playlist.

9. Engage with your audience

Businesses have a unique opportunity to engage and connect with their followers and buyers through social media. And, with 57 percent of consumers believing that a human connection will enhance brand loyalty and 58 percent believing that a human connection will increase the likelihood of a purchase, cultivating that relationship with your audience is crucial. Posing a question on one of your videos and putting it to the top of the thread as the creator is a terrific approach to show potential subscribers that you're active in the YouTube community. Posting a remark and pinning it to the top of the page not only shows that you've engaged with the platform but also encourages discussion on the video's subject. Follow the channels of your most devoted fans in addition to reacting to their remarks. Who knows, maybe one of your visitors may leave a terrific suggestion for a future video in the comments!

10. Use additional social media accounts to spread the word about your channel

Take advantage of the chance to promote your content on the other social media channels you use when you release a new video and encourage people to subscribe. It is based on the idea that if someone follows you on one platform and enjoys your posts, they may follow you on another — in this case, YouTube. An excellent illustration of this may be found in The Buttery Bros, a YouTube channel I often watch. These content makers specialize in fitness, particularly athletes competing in the CrossFit Games. They publish on Instagram whenever a new episode is released, as shown in the example below. With a fascinating image and a little information about the episode, the past informs the Instagram audience that a new episode has been released on YouTube. This post's artwork is similar to the YouTube thumbnail they use, going the additional mile to convey a subconscious feeling of brand recognition.

11. Share what you're working on next

If you think back to conventional television, one way to entice viewers to watch their favorite show the following week was to give them a sneak peek at what's coming up. For example, Game of Thrones was infamous for employing foreboding music and rapid cuts to grab the viewer and get them interested for the next episode. Your YouTube content has the potential to elicit the same level of interest.

Sharing what you're working on next if you want people to subscribe is a terrific approach to show them what they'll get if they do. It could be a terrific method to urge your audience to remain tuned for your next trip if you're developing a how-to series, for example. People are considerably more likely to recognize the value in subscribing if you leave them wanting more and tease what's coming next.

12. Tell a story

There's a reason why storytelling has endured for millennia. Although the medium has changed, the formula remains the same. Your viewers want to be educated and amused at the same time. They want to know that you understand what they're going through and that you can relate to them. People are drawn to stories when they recognize themselves in them. Rhodes is recognized as an expert in his profession and an actual human who people can identify to and root for, thanks to his concentration on delivering true stories about homesteading and including stories about his family. Consider the narrative you want to tell with your content. What knowledge do you have that you can share with the rest of the world? Is it possible to phrase things in a way that tells a story while also establishing trust? When it comes to understanding the world and passing on our experiences, we've been telling tales since the beginning of time. Take another look if you're reading this and don't believe you have a compelling narrative to tell. With billions of monthly visitors on YouTube, there's a significant potential that your narrative will resonate with people who could become your subscriber base.

Subscribers add value to your channel

Simply put, your YouTube subscribers are not just your die-hard fans, but they're also the first to view a new video when it's released, the first to engage with it; they're also the most enthusiastic about recommending it to others who share their passions. Increased YouTube subscriber numbers are essential to establishing success on the platform, focusing on community building. There are several subscriber milestones that you must meet to progress in your YouTube career. The number of subscribers will rise rapidly if you concentrate on producing valuable and entertaining content for a specific audience, but don't hesitate to experiment with new ideas. You never know what will resonate with your audience unless you try it. And if something doesn't work, your channel isn't over yet.

Chapter no. 4

YouTube stars are more influential Then other traditional celebrities.

YouTube producers are more influential than traditional celebrities among millennials who spend a lot of time viewing internet videos. Here, we compare and contrast the influence of YouTube personalities with that of TV, cinema, sports, music, and other celebrities. For many decades, television served as the principal source of news and entertainment. It was also how they were approached for marketing. Almost every commercial included a celebrity endorsing the superiority of a particular product or service. This is still true to some extent now. Neil Patrick Harris appears in Heineken Beer advertisements, and there is a slew of celebrities in Super Bowl commercials. However, the rise of social media, the declining popularity of television, and people's dislike of advertising lead to a re-definition of the term "celebrity." The ordinary people are now the ones who establish the trends and shape public opinion, and they're doing it on YouTube. As of 2015, millennials were the most significant consumer demographic, with $1.3 trillion in purchasing power.

Millennials are a popular target for marketers, yet they rarely watch television and are uninterested in what prominent celebrities say about products or services. They place the most trust in their social media tribes and peer-to-peer guidance. In a Defy Media survey, 63 percent of respondents aged 13 to 24 said they would try a brand or product advised by a YouTube video creator, compared to only 48 percent who said the same about a movie or TV celebrity. Businesses are taking note and turning to ordinary people rather than celebrities to reach out to millennials. Surprisingly, YouTube stars' influence on younger people extends beyond buying.

In 2014, Variety commissioned a survey of 13- to 18-year-olds in the United States to discover the most influential people in their lives. They were asked to rank 20 well-known people based on their approachability, genuineness, and other factors that the respondents considered essential parts of their overall influence. Popular YouTubers dominated the top five spots in the final list, with established celebrities like Jennifer Lawrence and Katy Perry settling for lower rankings. The magazine commissioned this investigation once more in 2015. The results, however, have remained consistent, with famous YouTube personalities taking the top six slots. So, why do YouTube personalities have a more significant influence on millennials and teens than established celebrities?

1. YouTube stars are better at developing relationships

People don't relate to traditional celebrities since they seem to operate according to their public relations methods rather than free will. It's sometimes difficult to tell where a beautifully prepared image ends, and the natural person begins. Inauthenticity is something that millennials abhor. By being friendly and creating intimate encounters with their viewers, YouTube stars, on the other hand, connect better with people. They aren't afraid to be wacky, hilarious, strange, or speak about sensitive and personal issues like sex, divorce, domestic abuse, or racism. According to a Google-commissioned study, 40% of millennial YouTube users believe their favorite video creators know them better than their friends, and 70% of teens believe they can relate to them better than traditional celebrities.

2. YouTube stars drive more engagement

It's challenging to picture contacting traditional celebrities and obtaining a personal response (rather than one delivered by a hired representative). On the other hand, YouTube stars respond to comments promptly, are approachable on social media, and hold frequent Q&A sessions with their audience, during which no question is off-limits. According to the same Google statistics, YouTube content creators' relationship with their fan base leads to better engagement. Videos generated by the top 25 YouTube stars receive three times the number of views, 12 times the number of comments, and two times the number of actions as videos created by mainstream celebrities (thumbs-ups, shares, clicks, etc.).

3. **YouTube personalities set trends and shape pop culture**

YouTubers, according to the majority of millennials, now set more trends than traditional superstars. 70% of YouTube subscribers believe that YouTube personalities influence and shape pop culture, and 60% of them say they would prefer to buy anything based on a YouTube star's recommendation over a TV or movie star's recommendation. In addition, several teenagers who regularly watch YouTube admitted in a study conducted by the University of Twente that they are interested "in what older YouTubers have to say about things" because it helps them shape their own opinions and worldview on specific topics such as design, beauty, games, relationships, and conflict management. Older generations, who are less exposed to YouTube culture and prefer traditional media such as TV and newspapers, where traditional celebrities still shape the debate, may be turned off by YouTube personalities' impact. However, it is at an all-time high among millennials.

4. YouTube Stars are Masters at building brands

When you're not around other people, your brand is your image, perception, and story. When we are not present, the producer of any form of online content lives on good feedback. They don't mind if the lighting is poor or a greater emphasis on quantity than quality. It's the chatter that counts.

If you've created a buzz, it signifies you've piqued your audience's interest. You can make money with promos and commercials because of the ease of speed, novelty, and technology. Producers can then reinvest their profits in the channel by upgrading their equipment or teaming with superior specialists to improve the overall experience. It amplifies your audience's direction and may result in increased traffic. This advantage over traditional stars is that their branding isn't associated with the most frequent possession of a Millennial — a smartphone. Commercials, sponsorships, and labeling are all critical to their companies. Oh! Of course, they have a face, a name, and a body. For Millennials, these are no-go areas. It is a one-of-a-kind battle. It's like fighting with a flamethrower in a stick fight.

5. YouTube Stars are pacesetters

70% of YouTube stars are expected to set trends and influence pop culture or the purchases made by Millennials. This truth may be called into question in the future if better search engines replace TVs and newspapers. It's on the high road with Millennials, though.

Why YouTube Stars Are More Influential Than Traditional Celebrities

You're in a coffee shop, and two of your buddies are sitting in front of you. A is on the right. A talk you about their day, inquiries about yours, and appears to be interested and attentive. Bis is on the left. B does not speak to you or interact with you in any manner while they are physically present with you. When you try to grab their attention, Despite this, B tells you how much they love and appreciate you from time to time, even if they're ignoring you. Who would you prefer to spend time with? In July 2016, Celie O'Neil-Hart, Content Marketing Manager, and Howard Blumenstein, Product Marketing Manager, published an article on why YouTube celebrities are more influential than traditional celebrities (Why YouTube Stars Are More Influential Than Traditional Celebrities). YouTube stars are represented by A in the preceding comparison, while traditional celebrities are represented by B. The fundamental explanation for the disparities is how everyone uses their particular celebrity in terms of image and connection to their supporters.

Traditional superstars gain notoriety by being "impossible to reach." You can't have their fancy clothes, money, beauty or talent, or, most importantly, their power. These superstars' success is based on audiences that aspire to have what they have, something they will almost certainly never achieve. Fans are entirely disconnected from the lives of these celebrities, despite their admiration for them. YouTube celebrities, on the other hand, appear to be admirable yet still approachable acquaintances. YouTube creators benefit from a video platform that allows them to interact directly with their audiences. Whether their films are brief or long, their primary goal is to develop a close bond with their viewers. YouTubers use the platform's ability to talk directly to an audience while maintaining a positive image. They don't just flaunt their personalities; they also demonstrate how proud they are of the minor oddities that set them apart from the rest of the world. Celebrities, in the traditional sense, desire to appear flawless. YouTubers strive to appear perfect in their flaws.

Viewers trust popular YouTubers for life advice, style advice, and everything else because of their apparent honesty. The genuineness of YouTube personalities is on their side. They have complete discretion over what they post and when they post it, with no apparent requirement for external approval. When they say something, it's them, not a PR or paparazzi, who say it. 7 out of 10 YouTube subscribers believe that YouTube creators influence and shape culture, and 6 out of 10 would rather listen to their favorite creator's recommendations on what to buy than their favorite TV or movie star (O'Neil-Hart &

Blumenstein, Why YouTube). This isn't to say that traditional celebrities should be avoided; it just means that we should take YouTube and other popular influencer platforms more seriously. Zoella, a prominent beauty guru with 11 million followers, released a video titled "February Favorites 2016" on March 6, 2016, in which she simply listed and detailed the products she enjoyed in February. A Knock Dream Journal, Divines Ol Shampoo & Conditioner, and Sophie Kinsella's novel "Finding Audrey" were among the products she listed. Google searches for these particular products increased within minutes of uploading this video, and the Knock Dream Journal soon sold out. Authenticity doesn't always sell, but it does on YouTube.

Between 2011 and 2016, Q2 traditional TV viewing by 18-24 year-olds dropped by more than 9 hours per week

Chapter no.5

More Views on YouTube for Free.

The answer is yes. When it comes to advertising, enlightening and entertaining audiences, YouTube is second only to Google in terms of popularity. More than 22 billion people visit YouTube each month, with an average session time of around 40 minutes. A lot of people utilize YouTube. In the same way that individuals have started to pay money to advertise their videos on YouTube, people have started to pay money for more views on their YouTube videos. People buy YouTube views in the hopes of deceiving YouTube's algorithms or persuading viewers that because so many others have watched their video, they should as well. There are a couple of issues with this strategy:

- YouTube's bot detection capabilities are improving all the time.
- Rather than counting views, the algorithms are focusing on user activity.
- It can be costly.

There is work involved in boosting your YouTube views for free, but if you do it correctly, you'll be rewarded with more views and an enhanced user experience, as well as the potential to extend your content. The network has the power to reach billions, whether you're sharing recipes, teaching people how to make moppet origami, or mocking presidents. So, how can you increase your YouTube views and attract more people to watch your videos? Here are 30 suggestions to help you do just that.

Get Views from YouTube's Organic Search Results

YouTube uses its algorithms for presenting the best and most relevant videos to consumers, similar to Google's search results algorithms. Consider what would happen if a blind individual was given the responsibility of categorizing content and deciding which content was the best. Does it appear to be difficult? Fortunately, YouTube's algorithm considers a wide variety of factors when determining which videos are the best and should show at the top of its search results.

- **Use Descriptive and Keyword Rich Titles**

Keyword research might come in useful here. In addition to providing keywords for the algorithm to use, a well-written and compelling title entices viewers and educates them about the substance of the video. You may use tried-and-true SEO methods like a keyword planner or other keyword tools for keyword research.

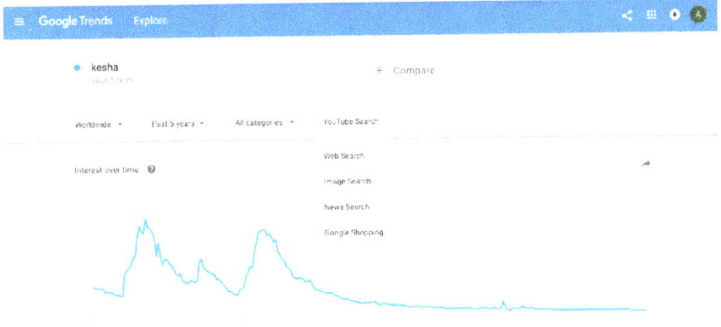

Go to keyword planner and pick YouTube search on the far right to see how popular a keyword is on YouTube. By telling consumers and search engines what your video is about, optimizing your video content for the correct keywords will help you gain organic views.

- **Have Quality and Keyword Rich Descriptions**

By describing the video, you can better educate search engines and viewers about your video. Your video's click-through rate and subsequently the number of views will increase since users will know what to anticipate. Try to stand out while being general; you want to pique people's curiosity while still attempting to rank for short-tail keywords. Use your descriptions to entice people above the fold and optimize them for the YouTube search engine like you would a conventional SEO meta description.

- **Use Tags**

Video tags on YouTube help viewers and the system understand what your video is about and what they may expect to see when they watch it. Including them, together with your film's description and title, should express its essence. Re-evaluate the value of long-tail SEO.

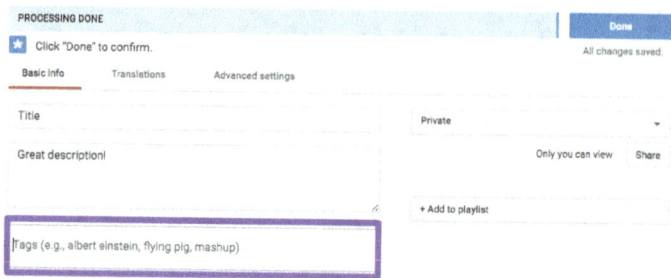

If you need help with keywords, use the keyword planner, as previously indicated.

- **Optimize Your Thumbnail Image**

Whether it's on the organic results page, the suggested videos area, or social media, your thumbnail image, like a hero image, may do wonders for raising your YouTube views. Use high-resolution graphics with readable and exciting typefaces, as well as facial close-ups if your video includes them.

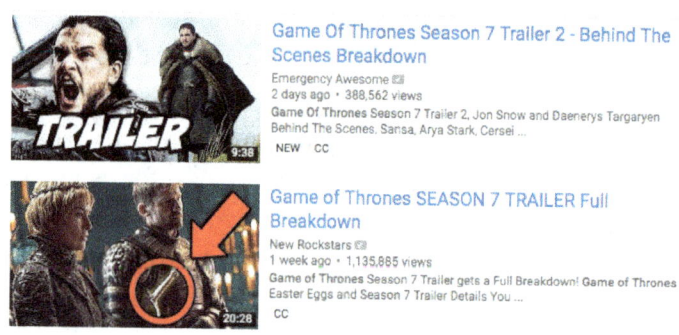

To increase your video views, make your thumbnail a visual match for your title and description.

- **Create Transcripts of Your Videos**

The ability of captions or transcripts of your videos to improve your YouTube rating has been hotly discussed. On the other hand, closed captions can assist increase YouTube views by catering to international audiences and the disabled. Ranking well in YouTube's organic results can dramatically increase your views and provide a long-term traffic source. Buying YouTube views may provide an immediate increase in views. Still, it's not a suitable long-term solution because YouTube's algorithms consider behavioral analytics a more critical ranking consideration.

Increase Views with Your Video Content

The most crucial aspect in determining how many views your video will receive is the content. Good content will lead to improved behavioral analytics, recognized by YouTube's algorithm, which will reward your video with higher organic search rankings.

- **Content that Educates or Entertains or Both**

Whether teaching people how to do or comprehend something or simply keeping them engaged and entertained, your video content should deliver value to the audience. When users find your content useful, they'll come back for more, increasing the number of views on your future video content.

- **Piggyback off of Viral Trends**

Make video content that capitalizes on already popular viral trends. You should capitalize on the market's inherent desire to examine material in the context of a viral phenomenon. All of the YouTube videos created in response to the United Airlines public relations disaster are a good example.

It's not always easy or viable to connect your video material to current events; nevertheless, if you can figure out a clever way to do so, you'll be able to increase your YouTube views with the support of a hungry audience eager for more trending contextual content.

- **Use Guest YouTubers**

Guest YouTubers, industry influencers, or people of significance with their following can do wonders for increasing your views, similar to guest posting for blog articles. Guest YouTubing can tempt your consumers with household industry names and bring a distinct and unique perspective to your business's area, similar to influencer marketing. You can establish a mutually beneficial relationship by including links to one of their movies or websites in your description.

Generating Views from the YouTube Platform

The goal of YouTube is to keep users on the platform. People that watch movies generate a lot of revenue for these companies via advertising. Because of this, there are several ways to keep active on the platform to increase your subscriber count and video views.

- **Create Video Content that Imitates Your Best**

"Good artists borrow, great artists steal," Picasso reportedly stated. While I would never advocate for copying in any way, Picasso's argument about successful YouTube videos rings entirely true. The Suggested Videos area, which shows on the sidebar and in a grid once a video has been completed, might be a goldmine for increasing your views.

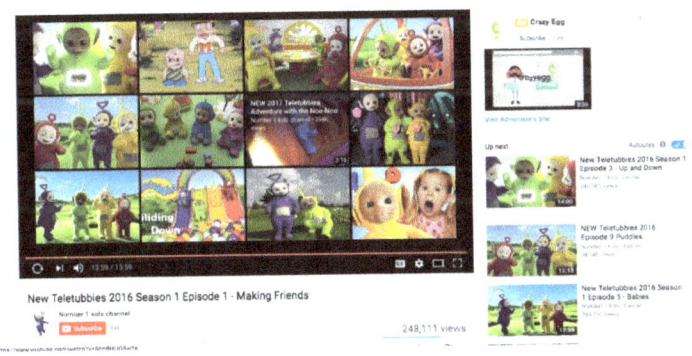

The video a user just viewed may have less to do with the initial query they entered and more to do with the relevancy of the video the user just saw. This is similar to how YouTube's algorithms work for organic results. As a result, the content shown at the end of a watched video will be comparable to what was just seen. By making your video relevant to other popular videos, you can improve the number of people who watch your YouTube channel and video. You can use similar keywords and descriptions to create video content that covers the same subject in a more engaging tone or with more information provided in an easier-to-understand fashion.

- **Use Cards**

You can use these YouTube optimization features to promote additional content in your video. You can use cards to:

- promote another video content
- increase channel subscribers
- donate to non-profit organizations
- drive traffic to your website • encourage visitors to take part in a poll

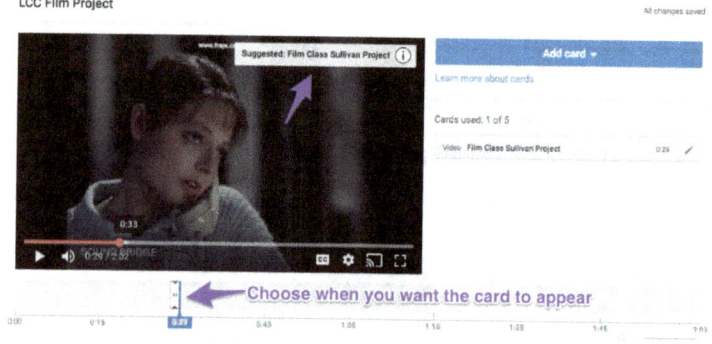

If you want to increase the number of views on your videos, you should utilize these cards to urge people to watch your less popular content and subscribe to your channel. Use your behavioral analytics to determine when users quit viewing your video and then use the card to ensure more people see it.

YouTube behavioral analytics give you a lot of valuable data and stats to help you make better decisions about getting more views on your videos.

- **Create End Screens**

End screens have the distinct ability to do a little bit of everything after your film. It's an opportunity to share all necessary information about your channel, other playlists, recommended videos, and your verified website to users who appreciate your material. Both optimization tools directly or indirectly enhance your YouTube views, whether you're gaining more subscribers or linking to your other videos. Go to your Video Manager, edit the video you wish to add end-screens to, and select End Screens & Annotations. You'll be able to add the other features from there. End screens are an excellent method to promote your material before YouTube's algorithms draw visitors away from your channel and videos by recommending other popular videos.

- **Promote a Marquee Video**

Having a highlight video on YouTube can assist promote your other videos as well as your YouTube channel. An excellent marker is to have at least 5,000 views on your video so that it appears in more search results owing to its already established popularity. As discussed previously, you can build cards, end screens, and other links to your other video material within your marquee video. Your marquee videos, similar to internal linking on websites, can help drive traffic and views to your lesser-known videos and channel in general.

- **Use Autoplay for your Embedded Videos**

When a video is embedded, Autoplay will start playing it automatically. You should use caution when doing so, as auto-playing movies may irritate some people. If the video material is instructive, it may be a good idea to use it because viewers can go right into the video that explains how to accomplish something. You may also set a playlist to play by embedding it using the same code automatically.

- **Create Playlists**

Make playlists for your videos so that visitors may watch them in order. After the first video has finished playing, your other videos will begin to play automatically, resulting in more views for each video played without the viewer having to leave the player. To raise the overall views for each playlist, you can embed it, upload it on your channel, or have users share it. Make each one unique, and the order in which they are played should give them flow and relevance. These are ideal for informative or amusing content that tells a story or delves into how several parts form a complete.

- **Be Present Within Your Niche Community**

Being an active part of your specialized group is one thing, but promoting oneself as an expert in your films is another. Comment on other videos and offer advice or feedback, and if there's video content lacking any essential information, link them to your content to supply them with further details. If you try to be as helpful as possible, you'll be rewarded with additional users, which will help you grow your subscription base and, ultimately, your video views.

Off-page View Boosters

YouTube is unique in that it can be found on a variety of social media platforms. With just a few clicks, it may be embedded and disseminated, sometimes virally. Here are some outside-of-YouTube strategies to increase your YouTube views.

- **Increase Your Video's SEO Ranking**

Traditional SEO is also a feasible option for increasing YouTube views, as videos can outrank the website on which they're featured in the search engines. Backlinks from video embeds are counted as backlinks, and in this situation, the links lead to the YouTube video, boosting its SEO rating. With a good SERP ranking, you may double the traffic to your video and double the number of viewers.

- **Post Links to Your Videos on your Profiles**

    Cross-platform promotion, particularly on YouTube, can help drive traffic to your site. You can reach your whole audience and direct them to your video by sharing links on other profiles. To increase your views, share the link as a post or include it in the description of your profiles. Additionally, by driving traffic to YouTube from your social media profiles, you'll gain favor with the algorithms by becoming the source of a large number of session beginnings, which are sessions that begin with specific videos on the platform. Sessions beginning on your video demonstrate that your video is driving visitors to YouTube, resulting in a higher organic rating and more appearances in suggested viewing sections.

- **Find Niche Communities to Share Your Video**

    You can distribute your content in several different ways. Different Reddit or Quora subreddits with themes relevant to your video's interests and target viewers are excellent places to share your material. Subreddits are also dedicated to simply sharing your video with YouTube lovers to increase its views, such as /r/GetMoreViewsYT. People post videos to this subreddit and vote on which ones they like most. Next week, the winner is stickied at the top of the subreddit for people to visit and watch. StumbleUpon and Pinterest are two other social bookmarking sites you can utilize to promote your films.

- **Find Influencers to Promote Your Video**

    Influencer marketing is quickly becoming a go-to method for big-name organizations to reach out to their target consumers. They have built-in audiences who re-share and promote their content, resulting in a viral increase in views. Social Media will help you find influencers in your field and reach out to them to promote your video content. Because viewers already follow these influencers and engage with the content they regularly give, a single share of your video can result in many views for your YouTube video and channel.

- **Embed Video Subscription**

While embedding your video will increase views, including a subscribe button to your channel will be incredibly beneficial in the long term. Subscribers account for almost half of a video's views; therefore, expanding your subscriber base will significantly increase video views. Follow these YouTube instructions to install the subscription widget and utilize it on pages with your video embedded.

- **Post About Giveaways and Promotions**

An excellent giveaway is something that everyone enjoys. Users will be directed to the video's YouTube page if you post about a promotion, giveaway, or raffle on social media. Tell your followers that the link to join us in the video's description. It will increase in views.

Remember to Be Patient.

It takes time to get a lot of views on YouTube. The platform has its own set of checks and balances to ensure that high-quality video material is available to its viewers at all times. Build an active subscriber base, and they'll account for the majority of your views.

Chapter no. 6

YouTube's impact on our society.

YouTube, a video-sharing website, has a much more significant impact on our culture than we might imagine. YouTube was created on February 14, 2005, and has had a significant impact on our society since then. Do you watch a YouTube video because the title is relatable or because it's funny? Probably the latter is unsurprising given how prevalent it is in our society to amuse one another by sharing films, images, or other forms of media with friends and family. Although some YouTube videos are created for fun purposes, many videos contain guidance for people looking for aid with various beauty how-and top tutorials. Famous beauty gurus such as Zoella, Bethany Mota, Rclbeauty101, and Meredith Foster share routines, hauls, monthly favorites, DIY's, expectations vs. reality, wardrobe suggestions, and makeup/hair tutorials with a focus on teen females.

Artists and bands with a YouTube account, particularly Vevo, play an essential role in contemporary society by releasing new singles or albums on their accounts, acquiring followers and reputation. Undiscovered singers frequently get attention on YouTube by releasing renditions of popular songs, which generates comments and, perhaps, leads to scouting. Justin Bieber, Carly Rae Jepsen, and Cody Simpson are three singers who started on YouTube and were discovered. A talent scout spotted

Justin Bieber and arranged for him to meet Usher. Justin Bieber supported Carly Rae Jepsen's single "Call Me Maybe" after tweeting to his over 18 million followers, "Call Me Maybe by Carly Rae Jepsen is the catchiest tune I've ever heard. Lol." Shawn Campbell, a record producer, discovered Cody Simpson when he was 12 years old and signed him to Atlantic Records. The impact of YouTube in the United States has allowed users to upload song covers or original content to their videos in the hopes of being noticed by companies.

Many Youtubers have simply uploaded a video to their channel without considering how many views and subscribers they will receive. YouTube impacts the US via streaming presidential elections, politics, commercials, and current events. Many YouTubers will publish videos with entertaining and superfluous thumbnails to attract viewers' attention, leading to a misconception of the actual video. The impact of publicly broadcasting videos on themes connected to global news, such as shootings, debates, and political campaigns, on viewers can be favorable or harmful. While some viewers will react positively to the news and appreciate the video's theme, others will react adversely by making superfluous and pointless comments, possibly targeting people in the video, ending in a cyber dispute. Some videos on political campaigns and debates can be deceptive to viewers if the uploader does not present the entire issue and only defends their side, resulting in a bit of video. Biased videos demonstrate the harmful impact of YouTube in our society by focusing on what the public wants to see rather than the biggest and most pressing issue. YouTube's influence on our society might have a beneficial or harmful impact due to the Variety of YouTube videos. Many YouTubers post videos in which they express their opinions on current events or issues. Whether the topic is pleasant or negative, viewers will most likely be impacted if they believe and agree with the video's content. Even if some YouTube videos are not intended to persuade or entertain viewers, the vast majority of them do.

The excellent or harmful effect of YouTube:

You've probably spent some time on YouTube if you're reading this. From how-to videos to political advertisements, the site has almost every video imaginable. The various films posted on YouTube by various groups demonstrate YouTube's influence on communication. As a result, it's critical to consider whether YouTube's media clout serves the greater good or obstructs society's ability to exchange intelligence information. According to a Helium.com story, YouTube is available to anyone, allowing for the upload of just about anything. Depending on the circumstances, the experience might be either favorable or unfavorable. For example, there are a variety of political advertisements on YouTube that address current concerns, prompting viewers to make their comments and igniting a creative debate that might be unpleasant. On the other hand, these concerns should not deter users from sharing on the site and how video material is distributed to viewers.

According to the Pew Journalism Research Center, around 21% of YouTube videos are tied to politics somehow. Politics is a popular topic since it allows for debate and discussion. The concept of communicating what interests you is a novel one that many people can relate to. Users also share what they watch on YouTube, resulting in a mash-up of videos spread throughout various social media platforms. In this approach, YouTube is viewed as a beneficial medium for sharing ideas and building online communities based on common interests. Several disadvantages may drive some people to reconsider sharing the videos they see on YouTube with others. However, an article on Teen Ink stated that so much free expression could cause controversy, as some people will use films to protest particular groups of people. It is considered a negative consequence because it may result in copyright breaches and censorship. As a result, a discussion has erupted over how filtering should be applied to certain films on YouTube. According to research in the Journal of Electronic Publishing, users need to keep sharing and distributing video content despite these challenges.

One's viewpoints can have a significant impact on how one interprets YouTube. Those who perceive YouTube as a platform to share and watch a wide range of videos on various topics appreciate the media influence it provides. However, other people believe that YouTube should be regulated to protect its integrity. It is simply a wrong thought in the minds of those who make it; it is not inherently harmful by nature. Consider how people choose to share what they learn or watch on YouTube to understand better how YouTube influences media.

Chapter no.7

Promote your YouTube channel for more views.

If you want to be seen on YouTube, you should use as many advertising strategies as possible. We'll go through each of these strategies to promote your YouTube channel and increase your popularity in depth below. These techniques are all fair game, whether you're just getting started or want to see your numbers rise even higher.

Increase the effectiveness of your YouTube strategy

To maximize your efforts with these guides, in addition to the 16 ideas below, make sure you're up to date on all things YouTube:

- Start a YouTube channel for your company and make it easier to manage and grow it.
- To make your videos stand out and be easily found on YouTube, it is essential to write compelling descriptions.
- SEO for YouTube — How to Rank Your Videos Higher — In recent years, YouTube has become one of the world's most popular search engines. By following these rules, you may ensure that you're meeting the needs of your audience.

- How to Boost YouTube Views using Hashtags – Make sure you understand how hashtags are used on YouTube so you get more views.
- How to utilize YouTube Analytics to improve the performance of your videos – Ensure that all of your efforts are successful, and identify areas where you can improve using good analytics.

Tips to promote your YouTube Channel

Create captivating, must-see titles.

When it comes to YouTube marketing, the presentation is everything. As far as the success of your video is concerned, the titles are essential. Your stuff should be seen as "must-see" or "meh." Your title is the first thing that a reader sees, so it's vital to grab their attention without resorting to clickbait. From the beginning, your audience wants to know what your film is all about. Take a cue from the likes of BuzzFeed and What Culture, two of the biggest names on YouTube. Listicles, question-based titles, or hyperbole are common ways to get more people to watch these flicks ("crazy," "...of all time"). Among the best examples of this is Athena X's workout videos. The programming on the channel manages to include relevant keywords in its names while also appearing conversational. The message here is that you should think about appealing titles instead of sticking with the first concept that comes to mind.

According to Tubular Insights, YouTube video names should be between 41 and 70 characters in length. For an engaging title, companies like CoSchedule's headline analyzer suggest a headline length of 55 characters. Although CoSchedule's tool isn't designed exclusively for video titles, it's great for coming up with YouTube-friendly names to help market your channel.

Make your films more visible by optimizing them

Here are some ideas to ponder: 70 percent of the top 100 Google search results include YouTube videos. Take a look for yourself. Google will return anything from YouTube for any given product or "how-to" inquiry. Search engine YouTube is the second biggest in the world. When it comes to searching for things and solving issues, people utilize YouTube much as Google. You should treat your YouTube videos like any other piece of content that has to be optimized for keywords or tags. Several recommended practices may increase your chances of being ranked highly on YouTube:

- Always include relevant keywords in titles and descriptions. Using a tool like Keywordtool.io, you may find keyword ideas.

- To assist YouTube in better understanding what your video is all about, include your goal keywords in your video. Backlink's Brian Dean recommends this.
- To rank videos in its search results, YouTube takes user interaction (such as the number of "likes," "comments," and "views") into account.
- To help YouTube figure out who your films should be presented to, use categories.
- As well as the categories, you may include tags in your videos for more information about your work on YouTube. Add as many tags as long as you don't exceed the number of tags allowed.

Don't keyword stuff, just like you wouldn't with your website's SEO. Use keywords only when they make sense, not just to have them.

Determine what your target audience desires.

Any form of material you publish should be by your audience's expectations. Before producing a blog post or filming a video, learn about your target audience and the kind of content they like.

If you're just beginning to advertise your YouTube channel, have a peek at your competitors or other video makers in your sector. Notice that which of their videos gets the most attention and involvement. Using this information, you may learn more about what your audience is interested in. If you've previously published videos, another option is to look at your YouTube Analytics. YouTube provides precise demographics, geography, interaction, and other useful statistics for your audience. Analyze how your videos stack up against other material you've produced using Sprout Social YouTube reporting.

Become a member of the community on YouTube.

Individuals on YouTube may interact by creating profiles, giving "likes," and leaving comments on one another's videos.

According to what we've heard, it's rather "social."

Like we stated before, YouTube looks favorably on any indicator of audience interaction. If nothing else, interacting with your subscribers will help you create a stronger connection with them. The time it takes to "like" a comment is even shorter than it takes to "pin" a comment. Several channels often reply to comments on their most recent uploads, for example. The author of the channel often contacts fans to show thanks and answer queries. Responses and engagement with your followers are the same on YouTube as on any other social media channel.

Make your thumbnails unique.

Using custom thumbnails to promote your YouTube channel is one of the easiest and most efficient methods. Think of your title and thumbnail as an enticing one-two punch. The thumbnail for each video on YouTube is automatically generated using a screenshot taken from the video itself. A fuzzy picture of you adjusting your camera or making a transition is what it often catches.

Isn't that a bad look?

In addition to making your videos more visually attractive, making your thumbnails indicates professionalism. Though they might be complicated in some instances, creating simple thumbnails is quite acceptable. Creating a template with a specific font and style to make it more uniform and on-brand is possible. An image creation tool like Canva makes this even more straightforward.

Cross-promote your own YouTube videos.

There's a strong likelihood that you're writing about the same things on YouTube. It's a good idea to cross-promote your earlier videos when it makes sense to do so. For example, you may add links in a video's description and urge viewers to check them out as a call-to-action. Although the sudden removal of YouTube's annotation tool may have disappointed some, providing a link in your description encourages people to watch your videos all the way through without clicking away.

Google search results that you want to target

As previously said, YouTube is crushing things when it comes to SEO. While you shouldn't create material solely for search engines rather than for humans, you should advertise your YouTube channel with SEO in mind. Search engine results pages tend to favor long-form (10+ minute) videos and product evaluations, as well as how-to guides and tutorials (SERPs). If you don't have a lot of video ideas, think about using your YouTube channel's marketing to capitalize on a trending term in your industry.

Organize a competition or a giveaway.

A giveaway is something that YouTube subscribers adore. If you want people to join your YouTube community, host a contest or gift. To make your competitions easier for your audience, ask them to like your video; please leave a comment on it and subscribe to my channel. We've put up a list of recommended practices for every social media contest.

- Make sure you're abiding by YouTube's rules.
- Give away a gift relevant to your brand: you want to attract people who aren't just looking for free stuff.
- Incorporate user-generated content and other non-traditional entrance requirements to become innovative.

The key is to limit the number of competitions you run on YouTube. Your time, money, and resources will be wasted if you don't know what you're doing is working. After you've completed one contest, take a look at your subscriber drop-off rate and engagement statistics. If you're not drawing engaged subscribers, you might as well be attracting people looking for free stuff.

- **Encourage others to watch your show.**

Creating a video series covering a common theme or topic is a smart strategy to promote your YouTube channel. Bon Appétit, a popular gastronomic channel with a large following on YouTube, features various series, including their recurring "From the Test Kitchen" episodes. Series are a win-win situation for both artists and fans. You don't have to wrack your head around ideas as a creator since you hold yourself accountable for creating new YouTube material. As a result, your subscribers will have a reason to return to your channel regularly.

- **YouTube videos can be embedded.**

Some of the best locations to promote your YouTube channel are outside of YouTube. Video content, for example, has been proved to enhance conversion rates and reduce bounce rates. Add a video to a product page or blog post to keep visitors on the page longer and more interested (like we did below). Consider any opportunity to direct your on-site (or social media!) visitors to your YouTube channel a win.

- **To arrange your YouTube videos, make playlists.**

Creating additional videos will make it more difficult for people to find what they're looking for in your channel. As a result, playlists are a must-have. In addition to classifying and promoting binge-watching on your channel, playlists also help you keep track of your content. The Beard brand's grooming channel, for example, has hundreds of clips that cover a wide variety of topics and is updated regularly. Users may quickly access relevant content on the channel's playlists without having to search for it.

- **Calls to action can help you get more people to take action.**

Since video material can generate an immediate and personal connection with the viewer, sometimes the best way to get your films noticed is to ask for involvement. Because not everyone who appreciates one of your videos will remember to like it or subscribe to it, it's becoming more customary to include these reminders in the video's description or in the video itself. There's no shame in explicitly asking for some love, especially if you're a new channel. An excellent method to keep the discussion continuing is to ask visitors to answer a question in the comments area or view another video. Links to other videos or an external website might be used as a call to action.

- **Try out live streaming.**

Live video, one of the most popular social media fads, is here to stay. With the rise of applications like Facebook, Periscope, and Instagram, more and more companies are jumping on the bandwagon. For years, YouTube has been airing live videos, but only lately has it acquired popularity. Please explore the most popular YouTube Live videos to learn how other firms use the platform to their advantage. Using YouTube Live, here are some examples:

- Webinars
- Live tutorials
- Q&A sessions
- Product demonstrations

Don't be concerned if your streams aren't as smooth as you'd like them to be. You never know what will happen, which is part of the live video's joy (and risk). Live video's rough, natural quality is precisely what makes it so appealing. Check out Google's introduction to live streaming for more information on how to get started with YouTube Live.

Collaborate with other artists and businesses.

Some of YouTube's most successful stars have grown their audience through collaborating with other users. You meet new folks every time you work with a new coworker. With the help of a well-known and trusted content producer, new viewers are more inclined to subscribe to your channel. When it comes to a successful YouTube partnership, finding the right partner is essential to success. For your video to look authentic, you want to collaborate with content producers with the same interests as your organization. An excellent example of creative cooperation that isn't overtly commercial is the BuzzFeed and Purina relationship.

For a charge, run a YouTube marketing campaign

With the rise of pay-to-play marketing in general, you have the option of buying YouTube advertising to boost your exposure. There are several ad types available on YouTube, including the following:

- Display advertisements: Only available on PC, these adverts appear in the right-hand sidebar of videos.
- Overlay ads are semi-transparent advertisements that appear at the bottom of a video. Only the desktop version is available.
- Before, during, and after a video, you'll see adverts in the form of skippable and non-skippable videos. Unlike non-skippable adverts, which must be seen fully, skippable ads may be skipped after only five seconds.

- Before a user may watch a video, they must see a non-skippable ad in the bumper. Typically, they persist for around six seconds.
- Cards that appear in videos relevant to the viewer are known as sponsored cards. Using them to promote your goods or other information is an option.
- For each ad campaign, you may utilize an existing video or create a new one. When you use an existing video, you may choose a clip that has proven successful in the past. An organically popular video may benefit from paid advertising, as long as it has a large following.
- A new video for your advertisements allows you to create a more concentrated and personalized product. For example, when creating advertising, you may include a customized CTA at the end that drives people to a particular website or video. Here you may learn more about YouTube's video ad types.

Share your YouTube videos on social media regularly.

It's no secret that video content dominates social media in terms of both engagement and performance. If you want people to follow your YouTube channel, you'll need to promote it regularly on social media. As soon as a video is online, be sure to let your social media followers know about it through Facebook, Twitter, Instagram, and LinkedIn. A sample or clip of your most recent work may be created for each social networking site. Sprout Social allows you to plan and cross-promote your content without switching between different platforms. With the help of Viral Post, for example, you can guarantee that your content goes live at a time when your social followers are the most engaged. We've come to the end of our tutorial on how to advertise your YouTube channel!

- How do you promote your YouTube channel on the Internet?
- Building a YouTube audience isn't something that happens by chance.
- And, yes, if your space is filled with competitors, it might feel like a slog.

You should always have many different advertising methods stashed away in case you ever need to use them. Even though some of the ideas above may need more time and effort than others, they will all help you attract more followers to your YouTube channel. Download our social media video cheat sheet to receive ideas for video at every stage of the marketing funnel if you're ready to ramp up your YouTube presence and start seeing accurate business results.

Why Use YouTube?

After YouTube, Google is the most popular search engine. YouTube publishes more than 100 hours of fresh material every minute of every day. A large audience may be reached quickly and easily by using this strategy, whether it's for advertising or teaching. The following are some of the reasons why YouTube is so popular:

Boost your SEO.

The most popular content format is video, which is frequently shared on social media. Because Google and other search engines favor video, publishing a video on YouTube with solid titles, descriptions, and tags is a terrific method to enhance your search engine rating.

Branding That Works

Video is a quick and effective way to get your message out. People respond well to visual signals, and video is an excellent way to capture the mood and physical characteristics of whatever you're selling.

The show, don't tell.

Videos are an excellent approach to demonstrate things that are difficult to convey in words. Demonstrate to your pupils via screen capture recordings, live demonstrations, or even a whiteboard drawing.

Increase the Number of People Who Hear Your Message

Besides being the world's most popular video-sharing site, YouTube also has the highest number of views per user. Look at your other Facebook and Twitter feeds and see how many videos you see there. How frequently do you get videos through email from friends and family? A video may be easily shared on the Internet.

You don't require a large budget.

While having some sorts of videos made by experts has its advantages, not every video requires a six-figure budget. You may quickly and effectively create compelling videos of lectures, presentations, and more with minimum video equipment.

Mobile-Friendly Video

With so many students owning smartphones, video is an excellent way to reach out to them. YouTube is well-suited to mobile devices, and the vast majority of students already use it.

Conclusion:

YouTube is a Google video platform founded in 2005 by Steve Chen, Chad Hurley, and Jawed Karim and purchased for 1.6 billion dollars by Google in 2006. Jawed Karim's "Me at the Zoo," which has over 82 million views, was the first video to be shared. The site has evolved significantly since then, and its current statistics are astounding.

YouTube in 2021, After Facebook, YouTube is the second most popular social network in the globe, with 79 percent of internet users claiming to have a YouTube account. Every month, about 2 billion people use YouTube, with several billion views (more than 82,000 videos viewed in one second), 70% of which are on mobile devices. Every day, 720,000 hours of video are added, or to 30,000 hours every hour. The platform is available in over 90 countries and 80 languages, making it accessible to 95% of the global Internet population. Because of YouTube's large audience, 62 percent of businesses use the platform to submit videos and receive more exposure. 90% of users have discovered a new brand due to the platform, significantly since ad exposure has increased to 95%.

Many people are getting their feet wet on this platform by creating original material. Since last year, there has been a 40% rise in the number of channels making six-figure incomes and a 75% increase in the number of channels with more than one million members. Even if you don't know how to operate a computer, YouTube is simple to use. Do you still have questions about how to utilize this social networking platform? Don't worry; plenty of online tutorials will show you how to submit a video and much more. With YouTube, you can quickly distribute a large amount of information to a large number of people. You can also use entertainment to convey information. This could take the form of:

- Videos
- Music
- Comedy Sketch
- Video Animation

You can now submit YouTube stories, polls, and post updates, just like on other social media networks like Instagram, which will help you engage your audience significantly. You may, for example, conduct a poll to determine which topic your viewers would want to see next, which not only engages your audience but also allows you to learn what they want to visit from your channel. Backlinks from YouTube can assist you in improving your SEO. These backlinks can be produced by including a link to your website on your profile page and in the descriptions of each video you upload to your channel. By displaying your website link in various parts of your channel, you will raise awareness of your website and, as a result, increase traffic to it. Nowadays, YouTube is a very famous social networking site. It's great for personal usage, but it can also develop a brand for enterprises. Your films will appear not only on YouTube but also in other search engines such as Google. Are you considering using YouTube for personal or professional purposes? Continue reading because we'll explain both viewpoints in this chapter. YouTube allows you to upload and view videos for free. It allows you the freedom to try things out and see if they work for you without worrying about the costs. YouTube Premium, on the other hand, was recently introduced. YouTube Premium is a premium subscription that allows you to watch videos without advertisements, play videos in the background, and watch videos even when you're not connected to the Internet. It also lets you view original YouTube programs and movies and access YouTube Music Premium (a streaming platform).

As far as posting videos to your YouTube account, it doesn't matter if you have a Premium or a free account. YouTube is a place where you may earn money for watching other people's videos. To generate money from your videos, you'll need a Google AdSense account. You've got a Google AdSense account, but you're not sure what to do with it? You may register a new Google AdSense account if you have a YouTube channel. There are several methods to generate money on YouTube besides Google AdSense. The following strategies may be used to achieve this goal:

- Affiliate Links
- Sponsorships
- Merch and Products
- Selling Digital Products
- Offer Services
- and much more

This book is part of an ongoing collection called "Social Media Influence."

1. Increasing your Social Media Influence on Facebook.
2. Increasing your Social Media Influence on YouTube.
3. Increasing your Social Media Influence on WhatsApp.
4. Increasing your Social Media Influence on Instagram.
5. Increasing your Social Media Influence on TikTok.
6. Increasing your Social Media Influence on Snap Chat.
7. Increasing your Social Media Influence on Reddit.
8. Increasing your Social Media Influence on Pinterest.
9. Increasing your Social Media Influence on Twitter.
10. Increasing your Social Media Influence on LinkedIn.

Please check out Amazon for more books in this collection.

Author Bio

Aaron Cockman. Aaron enjoys reading and learning more about being profitable on social media, so she decided to write about something she is passionate about. More books will come in this collection, so follow her on Amazon for more books.

Thank you for your purchase of this book.

I honestly do appreciate it and appreciate you, my excellent customer.

God Bless You.

Sherry Lee.

www.ingramcontent.com/pod-product-compliance
Lightning Source LLC
Chambersburg PA
CBHW070301220526
45465CB00004B/1692